STUDY THE BIBLE

Six Easy Steps WORKBOOK

Second Edition

Dennis C Stevenson Jr

www.dennis-stevenson.com

Copyright © 2023

ISBN: 9798987505731

Lesson Plan

01 **What is the Bible?**
How you view the Bible dictates how you study it

02 **Choosing the right kind of study**
There are many ways to study the Bible.

03 **Foundations of Textual Study (1)**
Tools to help you understand what the passage is trying to say

04 **Foundations of Textual Study (2)**
Understand how words impact the meaning of the passage

05 **Applying what you learn**
The study is incomplete until you apply it to your life

06 **The Six Easy Step Method**
An overview of the Six Easy Steps study method

07 **Bible Study Resources for You**
Choosing the right resource can make a difference in your study

08 **How to Start a Study**
Learn how to prepare and orient yourself for study

09 **How To Do a Chapter Study**
The Six Easy Step method applied

10 **How to Finish Your Study**
Summarize your learning and wrap up the study

About this Study Guide

Studying the Bible is a core activity of the healthy Christian life.

From the earliest days of the church, the model has been for Christians do dig into God's Word to understand how to live their lives (Acts 17:10-11).

Scripture itself is identified as the final source for establishing right thinking, exposing error, applying correction and instructing the believer in right living (2 Timothy 3:16).

Despite the scriptural imperative, most adult Christians have not been taught the fundamentals of how to study the Bible.

This instructional guide, intended for normal believers, will introduce you to the basic skills needed to study the bible.   It lays a foundation of knowledge which can be expanded later with more in-depth levels of study.

01
What is the Bible?

How you view the Bible dictates how you study it

How we view the Bible drives how we study it

How would you read the Bible if it were ...

A Newspaper

____

____

A Novel

____

____

A Textbook

____

____

A Fortune Cookie

____

____

Everyone has an opinion about the Bible.

We all think of it in a specific way. Perhaps it's something that was modeled for us when we were younger or impressionable. Maybe it's something that we picked up from our peers or those around us. It could be that we pieced together our thoughts about the Bible from bits and snatches at church. For some, we have no idea what to think about the Bible and just make it up as we go along.

These opinions we bring with us are not free. In fact, they have a real impact on how we view the Bible and what we expect from it. From instilling reverence to determining what we choose to read to impacting how we understand it, our opinions are vitally important.

Before we begin, we need to look at these opinions about the Bible.

The Bible is communication from God

Psalm 119:11 – By knowing God's word (memorizing it), we can avoid sinning and live a life pleasing to God.

Psalm 119:105 – God's word provides direction and instruction for living.

Proverbs 30:5 – God's word is pure and untainted. It serves as a shield for those who trust in God.

John 6:67-68 – Peter recognized that what Jesus was saying was different than everyone else and the key to life (eternal).

Acts 6:7 – When the Word of God increased (was presented more boldly, more often), the church grew.

Hebrews 4:12 – The word of God has power and effect in our lives.

Traditionally we say, "the Bible is the Word of God."

This statement is foundational to our understanding of the Bible and defines its priority in Bible study.

In everyday conversation we use words to communicate to each other. God chose to use the same communication and expressed Himself in words – which we have today as the Bible.

God is the author of the Bible

The Bible was "breathed out" by God through human hands.

2 Peter 1:19-21 - The Holy Spirit was the motive force in its creation.

2 Timothy 3:16 - God breathed, profitable to define truth, identify error, correct wrong thinking, leading back to the right path.

Even though as many as 39 individual people are attributed as having written books, God is the ultimate author. The verses in 2 Peter and 2 Timothy make it very clear that God was present in the writing. "men spoke from God as they were carried along by the Holy Spirit." Here we see 2 members of the trinity involved in the writing of the scriptures.

The beauty of God's authorship of the Bible is that He allowed the individual people to express His message in their own voice, using their own unique style and words. Read a passage in the gospel of John and compare it to a passage in Hebrews, 1 Corinthians or Isaiah. They all sound very different. That's because different people were involved with God to put the words down.

Because God is the ultimate author, we see, through study, that the Bible is consistent and has one clear message that flows from Genesis to Revelation.

We find no error in the Bible

Doctrine of Inerrancy:

The teaching that the Bible is without error.

A doctrine is a teaching that is held to be true, often the foundation of a system of belief or faith.

The Bible is inerrant

Inerrant means "without error". Since the Bible is the Word of God, it carries the character and nature of God (God cannot speak contrary to His nature). Since God is true, complete, and trustworthy, His Word bears these same distinctions.

ALL of the Bible is inerrant – it does not "contain" the Word of God; it IS the Word of God. If some of it is not trustworthy, then none of it can be trustworthy and all of it is under a cloud of doubt.

Inerrancy applies to the original writing of the Bible. These originals have been, through the providence of God, carefully copied and maintained. They give us the manuscripts we have today, which are the basis of our English translations.

The Bible is our authority

Everywhere and every time the Bible speaks, it speaks with the words and voice of God.

What the Bible says is God saying it. Since God is the author, and is in control of what the Bible says, we give the words of the Bible the same weight and authority as if God sat down with us and said the words directly to us.

There is no authority over God (Romans 13:1). He is the ultimate authority and is above every other authority that we will encounter or can imagine. All authority flows from God, and His word is the voice of that authority.

Everything the Bible says is with the authority of God!

What is our proper relationship to the Bible?

Psalm 1:1-2 - The Old Testament extols the person who lives by obeying the Word of God

2 Timothy 2:15 – Our right relationship is to study God's word – so that we handle it rightly

If you want to hear God speak to you, read your Bible. If you want to hear God speak audibly, read out loud!

Meaning & communication

The purpose of communication is to deliver a specific message from a sender (speaker) to a receiver (listener or reader).

The message is determined by the sender. It is not appropriate for the receiver to try to determine the message.

Any deviation from the sender's intention in the receiver's understanding is called "miscommunication".

The Bible is God's Word to us; therefore, it has a specific meaning.

2 Peter 1:16-21 – The Bible has no private interpretation (hidden meanings, custom messages)

Each passage has one meaning, although it may have several implications (these are not the meaning), and many applications.

What it means "to me"

It's common and familiar to talk about what the Bible means "to me". As a student of the Bible, this is not a proper approach. God says the same words to everyone, with the same meaning.

The message of the Bible is the message. Period. How a person chooses to apply that message varies from person to person. But the meaning remains the same for everyone.

The Bible impacts your life right now!

It is not enough to know the truth about the Bible. For the truth to have any impact, it must affect the way you live your life. The impact of the truth is directly proportional to how much it affects you and the way you live.

Do you show respect to your Bible that matches your reverence for its contents?

____

How often do you read the Bible? Is it enough?

____

____

Do you understand what it says; are you striving to go deeper?

____

____

In what areas of your life do you need to begin to obey what you read in the bible?

____

____

02
Choosing the right kind of study

There are many ways to study the Bible.

Bible study is for everyone!

Most believers want to study the Bible but have no specific idea of what that means or how to go about it.

Christian bookstores are full of books about "Bible Study" and even provide Bible study tools. But the average person is more confused by the options than clarified. Where to begin? Which method to pick? What is the "best study" available?

In church believers might hear about others who are studying the Bible. It could seem complicated or scholarly. They might even conclude that since they haven't gone to Bible School, they don't have the skills to study the Bible.

The truth of the matter is that there are many different methods of studying the Bible. Some are so simple that anyone could do it. Others are more complicated and would benefit from instruction or specific training.

The bottom line is that no believer should ever be excluded from studying the Bible. In writing to his partner Timothy, the Apostle Paul says, "study to show yourself approved." He doesn't put any restrictions or limits on it. Just study. Do what you can with the skills you have!

This lesson focuses on understanding different kinds of Bible study – and you will be able to start with at least one of them today.

Different Bible studies for different reasons

Not all types of study are created equal.

Not all types of study are appropriate for every situation or circumstance. For the believer, understanding the types of study and appropriate use is critical to spiritual development.

Some types of study are better suited for beginners and other types are better suited toward more mature believers. But that doesn't change the fact that studying the Bible is right for <u>all</u> believers. No one gets an excuse not to study the Bible.

The key for you is to begin with the kind of study which is best suited to your level of maturity and skill. Then progress from there. In a year, or 5 years time, you should want to be ready for more in-depth study. That is the natural path of development. – from the simple to the more mature.

Milk vs. Meat

Hebrews 5:12-14 – The writer expected that at this time the readers should be mature and able to handle spiritual "meat". Instead, they were immature and could only handle spiritual "milk".

1 Corinthians 3:2-3 – Paul gave the Corinthians basic., or "milk," level teaching because that was all they were able to handle.

Study for the right reasons

2 Timothy 2:25

Do your best to present yourself to God as one approved, a worker who has no need to be ashamed, rightly handling the word of truth.

It is vitally important that when you study the Bible, you do so for the right reasons. Studying is not a badge of honor or status. It does not earn you points with God. The King James bible translates "do your best" as the word "study" and suggests the idea of preparing for a test or an exam.

Paul describes the life of study as a desire to please God. It is the way to live a life that results in the divine pronouncement "Well done, good and faithful servant!" This is a life of which God approves. One that is conformed to His values and demonstrates the fruit of the Spirit (Galatians 5:22-23).

For the Christian who studies and understands what God wants and expects of him or her, there is no shame. Paul suggests that there will be some Christians who will stand before God and leave ashamed that they didn't please Him more. These will be the Christians who did not do their best.

Different types of Bible study

The remainder of this lesson will look at the different types of study which are available to the Christian. You can see from the list to the right that there are many different options available.

From this list, you will undoubtedly be able to find one or more options which will be suitable to you in your walk with Christ. What's more, this list should also challenge you to grow and be able to take on more and different types of study.

Our goal as believers is to continually progress from a simple (milk) understanding to a more mature (meat) understanding of God's word.

Memorization

Meditation

Reading

Textual Study

Topical Study

Systematic Study

Memorization

Psalm 119:11

I have stored up your word in my heart, that I might not sin against you.

The simplest kind of studying the bible is memorizing it. The Psalmist says it best... I have memorized God's word so that I will not sin against God. Knowing what God expects is the first step to pleasing Him.

By memorizing God's word, I guarantee that I have it with me wherever I go. This means that whatever my circumstances, I can connect with what God has said:

- When I am tempted to sin – God's word will point out the right path
- When I need encouragement, I remember who God is and what He has already done.
- When I need to be reminded of who I am in Christ, I can focus on what God says
- When I need to know the right thing to do, I remember God's wisdom

Memorization works best with scripture that has clear meaning. It does not provide any real mechanism to understand more complicated passages. The point of memorization is to bring God's word to mind and focus on what He has said.

Biblical Meditation

Biblical meditation is about filling your mind with God's word.

Biblical meditation is simply thinking about, concentrating on, considering and pondering God's word. The best passages are often those which are image-oriented, or which have a clear message.

Biblical meditation works very well in conjunction with memorization. This makes meditation mobile. However, you can also meditate on a passage of scripture that you have just read (but not yet memorized).

The point of Biblical meditation is going over the scripture again and again. The word picture is like that of a cow chewing its cud. Just when you think you're done, go over it again... and again!

Joshua 1:8
This Book of the Law shall not depart from your mouth, but you shall meditate on it day and night, so that you may be careful to do according to all that is written in it. For then you will make your way prosperous, and then you will have good success.

Philippians 4:8 Finally, brothers, whatever is true, whatever is honorable, whatever is just, whatever is pure, whatever is lovely, whatever is commendable, if there is any excellence, if there is anything worthy of praise, think about these things.

Bible Reading

Through the Bible in a year

Chronological Bible

Through the NT in a year

Psalms & Gospels

Proverb a Day

Accelerated plans

Bible reading is a simple form of the next type of study we will consider: Textual Study. But it is a common, and valuable study tool for the believer.

The point of reading the Bible is to understand what it has to say. Let's face it, if we don't know what God has said in the Bible, we will have a very difficult time doing what it says.

The key to reading the Bible is to have a plan. There are lots of plans available that could provide structure and guidance to your Bible reading time. Pick one, based on what might interest you, or how much time you might have. The entire Bible can be read aloud in about 75 hours. So, it's much more accessible than you might think.

As you are reading the Bible, remember, these are God's words for you. Pay attention and listen to what they have to say.

Textual Study

Textual study is the foundational process to learn and apply God's truth to my life.

The purpose of this study method is to understand what God's word communicates to people (in general) and me (in particular). This is probably what most people think of when they hear the phrase "study the Bible".

In general, textual study follows this pattern:

- What does the text mean (original author to audience)?
- How does it apply to me (general vs. personal)?
- What must (should) I do?

Subsequent lessons will dive into how to pursue this method.

Textual study is critical for the "right handling of the Word of God." (2 Timothy 2:15) It focuses on understanding what God has said. It also demands application in our lives.

In 2 Timothy 3:14-17, the Apostle Paul describes the impact of scripture in the life of his protégé Timothy. Paul says that from Timothy's earliest days the scripture was preparing him for salvation. Now that he is saved, scripture has the effect of teaching truth, exposing error and providing correction back to the right path.

The goal of studying scripture is that the man or woman of God is complete, lacking nothing, and prepared for every good work.

Topical Study

Topical study is like textual study in many ways. It is primarily interested in understanding what God's word has to say. However instead of focusing on a specific passage or section of scripture, it picks a word or a topic and considers it throughout all of scripture.

This approach considers all the references to the word or topic and identifies what scripture teaches in each passage. This learning is then assembled, in a mosaic form, to create a fuller understanding of that given topic.

Some common topics might be:

- Love
- Grace
- Forgiveness

Topical studies strive to rightly handle God's word. So, it is crucial that for each passage being considered, the student must take the time to understand the author, audience and the context of the passage. Only in doing this can we properly understand what the author is trying to communicate and gain the correct understanding.

Once a topical study has been completed, the student will have a very detailed understanding of the word or topic. However, this understanding must be handled correctly. It cannot be simply injected into any passage that references the topic. Once again, context will be used to determine which aspects of the meaning are appropriate.

Systematic study

OLOGY = The study of...

Theology Proper: God the Father
Bibliology: the Bible
Christology: Jesus Christ
Pneumatology: the Holy Spirit
Anthropology: Man/humanity
Hamartiology: Sin
Soteriology: Salvation
Ecclesiology: the Church
Angelology: Angels
Satanology: Satan
Demonology: Demons
Eschatology: End times

The systematic study topics are often called "doctrines" and represent the foundational truth statements of the Christian faith.

Systematic theology breaks God's word into different topics and identifies the truth about those topics. It also defines how those topics relate to each other. The primary focus here is around organizing knowledge and truth into unambiguous statements. In many ways it brings a scientific-like discipline to studying what God has to say.

A systematic study is like a word or topical study in that it uses the entire Bible to develop the truth-statements about each of the systematic topics. In the same way, systematic study must continue to understand the author, audience and context to establish the meaning of what is being said in each referenced passage. For this reason, learning textual study is critical to understanding a systematic study.

The Bible impacts your life right now!

If the Bible is the word of God, then it must continually impact our lives and the way we live.

Which of the study methods above have you begun to use, used regularly, mastered?

____

What distractions lead you away from studying the Bible?

____

____

What lies do you believe that lead you away from time studying the Bible?

____

____

What one bold change do you need to make in your approach to studying the Bible?

____

____

03
Foundations of Textual Study (Part 1)

Tools to help you understand what the passage is trying to say

Understanding the Big Picture

Author

What do we know about the person who wrote this?

Audience

What do we know about the recipients

Literature Style

What does the style of literature say?

The beginning of every Bible study is understanding the big picture.

The Bible doesn't exist in a vacuum. It always comes with context and a very specific setting. This has a tremendous impact on our overall understanding of any given passage.

Who wrote it? To whom were they writing?   What style of writing did they use? These are critical opening questions for the Bible student. And despite how you might feel about these questions now, they can be answered relatively easily and will deliver a great insight on any passage.

The beginning of any Bible study is generally to take a step back and consider the big picture before diving into the details. Typically, this means reviewing the entire book of the Bible to obtain the correct context for the passage of interest.

Discover the Author

The first task of any Bible student is to understand what the author communicated to their audience.

Begin by identifying the author. Who were they? What do we know about them, and how does it give us insight into what they are saying? What is their status, position, role? What kinds of topics or issues do they want to address? Is there something that they want to accomplish that we should bear in mind?

The author is the first critical piece to being able to understand what God has to say to us.

Following is a short list of different books of the Bible. List out what is known about the author and how it can affect your study.

Genesis:

____

Judges:

____

Psalms:

____

Isaiah:

____

John:

____

Ephesians:

____

2 Peter:

____

Identify the Audience

To whom was this written? The identity of the audience gives invaluable clues to the meaning of the passage.

Often the passage, or the larger book, will provide clues about the initial readers of the message. What do we know about them, their relationship to the author, the specific circumstances they were facing, and their relationship to God?

If the audience is a troubled church, we'd expect one kind of message. If the audience is the rebellious nation of Israel, we would expect something different. Discover the audience as a clue to what God is trying to say.

Following is a short list of different books of the Bible. List out what is known about the initial readers and how it can affect your study.

Genesis:

____

Judges:

____

Psalms:

____

Isaiah:

____

John:

____

Ephesians:

____

2 Peter:

____

Genres of Literature

History

Tells a story of what happened. Can be objective, or a first-hand perspective. Tends to focus on a general, not specific, audience. Is more focused on background and education.

Poetry

Uses picturesque language to communicate feelings or an internal state. Tends to be more personal than educational

Letters

Letters written from one person to another, or a specific group. Can be both educational and teaching, or very personal depending on the author's message.

Gospels

Similar to history in that it tells a story, but in this case the subject of the story is Jesus' life and death. Gospel literature points directly to salvation.

Prophecy

Communication coming directly from God. Often involving events which have not yes happened. Often based on imagery or graphic word pictures.

Wisdom

An ancient form of literature that focused on communicating wise teaching through a specific format and pattern of writing.

What Type of Literature?

A poem is different from a letter which is different from an historical account.

Different authors use different genres or styles of literature to communicate their message. This choice is just as important as the specific words they choose to use. Sometimes the purpose of the book itself determines the genre. Other times the specific message is best communicated in a certain style.

Sometimes, different books of the bible will employ different literary styles or conventions within a given book (poetic outburst, parable, genealogy...). Even these changes provide clues to what the author is trying to say.

Following is a short list of different books of the Bible. List out what is known about the type of literature and how it can affect your study.

Genesis:

____

Judges:

____

Psalms:

____

Isaiah:

____

John:

____

Ephesians:

____

2 Peter:

____

You took me out of context!

Modern communication is characterized by behaviors that work against a proper understanding of the Bible.

These skills and behaviors are commonly used by many people as techniques for managing the onslaught of information in our society today. They are largely aimed at filtering out information we don't need to pay attention to.

However, when reading and studying, the Bible we need less filtering, not more filtering. So, it is important for the Bible student to avoid these techniques.

Skimming:

____

____

Partial Reading:

____

____

Sound bites:

____

____

Multi-tasking:

____

____

Bible Study Reading Skills

Studying God's Word requires an approach which ensures the correct context is set and the proper message is received.

The Bible student must develop new skills and techniques to properly handle God's word. These skills are focused on deep comprehension and focus. They help us tune out distractions which would otherwise interfere with our understanding.

At first, these techniques might seem strange and unfamiliar. With repetition and practice, they will become more comfortable.

Deep reading:

____

____

Reading through:

____

____

Finding context:

____

____

Dedicated focus:

____

____

It's all about the Context

Every time we study the Bible, the passage must be understood in the context of how it was being communicated by the author to the audience.

"A young believer looking for wisdom in a difficult circumstance opened their bible at random and picked a verse to read: Matthew 27:5b. Shocked they opened to another random verse: Luke 10:37b. Completely shaken they tried one more time: John 13:27b."

Did this experience yield "rightly handling the word of truth"?

____

____

Read Luke 5:17-26

What do we know about the context?

____

____

____

How does context help us understand the Pharisee's charge?

____

____

How does context help us understand Jesus' response?

____

____

The Bible impacts your life right now!

How are you tempted to shortchange your study of the word of God?

"Because I'm not skilled, I won't even try."

"Because I don't have a lot of time, I won't use good technique."

"I only want to study if I get feel-good messages in return."

"I only want to study on my own terms."

"I only want to study so I can get head-smart."

Something else?

04
Foundations of Textual Study (Part 2)

Understand how grammar impacts the meaning of the passage

Using Tools of Literature

Paragraphs

Contain one key thought or idea which is supported by several sentences.

Sentences

Come in different kinds which can be used to create different meanings.

Words

Key words can unlock meaning and show us what the author wanted to say.

Because the Bible is delivered to us as literature, we must use the fundamental tools of literature to discover what it means: Paragraphs, Sentences & Words.

As adults we generally understand the written word. But when it comes to studying the Bible, it is useful to extend our normal comprehension so we can dig deeper and understand more of what God has to say.

The necessary tools are not difficult, we were probably taught most of what we need in middle school or Jr. High. But the odds are we haven't practiced these skills for a long time. They are there, but rusty.

Studying the Bible benefits the most from practice. Using the skills and tools over and over makes them much easier to use. Don't let the initial unfamiliarity prevent you from getting started.

Paragraphs as Building Blocks

When translating into English, most translators apply standard conventions of English grammar – including the use of paragraphs – even though they do not exist in the original manuscripts. This helps English readers properly understand what has been written.

A paragraph consists of several sentences that are grouped together. This group of sentences together discuss one main subject. In U.S. formal academic English, paragraphs have three principal parts. These three parts are the topic sentence, body sentences, and the concluding sentence. *http://lrs.ed.uiuc.edu/students/fwalters/para.html*

When you encounter a paragraph in the biblical text, *it is appropriate to identify the main subject*. What is the paragraph about?

- The paragraph may not lead with the topic sentence, so you may need to search for it.
- The topic may be implied or pointed to, but not explicitly stated.

Once you have identified the subject of the paragraph, you have a good idea what he author was trying to communicate. Each of the sentences should then relate to or support the main idea in some way or another.

Paragraphs are great building blocks of comprehension. In a larger passage, paragraphs are a great way to break down what has been written into more understandable chunks.

Identifying Paragraph Points

Test your understanding of paragraphs with this exercise. Don't worry about finding the "right answer". This is more about practicing how you understand paragraphs.

People who worry about finding the "right answer" tend to freeze up on exercises like this. Let the text itself guide you to the answer and you will find good answers.

Read Acts 6:1-6 and answer the questions below

What is the topic sentence?

____

____

What are the supporting or body sentences?

____

____

____

What is the concluding sentence or result?

____

____

____

Different Kinds of Sentences

Not all sentences are created alike. Sentences can have very different structures – which results in very different kinds of meaning.

Declarative: Makes a statement. This is a declarative sentence.
Genesis 1:1

____

____

Interrogative: Asks a question.

John 6:42:

____

____

Romans 6:1

____

____

____

In some cases, the question asked presumes an answer. In the John passage above, the question is rhetorical in the affirmative. The Romans passage is a setup for an emphatic negative answer.

Different Kinds of Sentences

Just about every sentence you encounter will fall into one of these 4 types. You can use the sentence types to help you zero in on meaning.

Imperative: Gives a command or makes a request. Common in dialog but can be used in other settings. Imperative statements should really grab our attention because they call for action from the reader.

Joshua 1:6:

____

Romans 12:1-2

____

____

Exclamatory: Expresses strong feeling, emotion or opinion. Exclamatory sentences add emphasis to the point being made.

Psalm 23:1

____

1 John 3:1

____

Using Sentences in Bible Study

There is no limit to the ways different types of sentences are used in the Bible. The attentive student will, however, begin to identify patterns that aid in determining meaning.

When reading the epistles (letters in the New Testament), it is common to look for imperative sentences which issue commands that must be obeyed. Finding a commend in the middle of a long paragraph can bring focus to a passage which is otherwise confusing. A common practice is to highlight imperative sentences in a passage to help focus on the areas that demand special action.

Another common Bible study technique is to look for questions and answers. In dialog, these are often important interactions. In more narrative styles, these are the kinds of conventions that point to key messages in the text.

Exclamations are also a hint that something important is happening. They show emotion and intensity on the part of the author or speaker. Being able to identify these sentences can often lead to the emotional point of what is being said.

A Look at Grammar and Structures

Since Biblical communication is made of words, their meaning and structure have a significant impact on the message being sent.

You are encouraged to become familiar with words which tend to be associated with key points or meanings in the text of a given passage. These words are common ones across the English language and create a direct method to identify where key points are being made.

Often Bible study is about identifying where conclusions are being drawn or where contrasts are being made. In these places you can more easily focus on the point the author was making.

In general, this technique focuses on the connecting words in the English language. These connecting words are used to link sentences together in logical ways — and it is this logical linking that reveals what is being communicated.

The most common connections are **summarization**, **conclusion** and **contrast**.

Summarization shows where the author is distilling the essence of previous points in a concise format. In conclusion statements, the author brings together several ideas and provides the logical outcome of the ideas. In contrast, two ore more ideas are compared and shown to be different or opposite.

Conjunctions as Linking Words

AND – More of the same

Matthew 6:11-13:

____

____

____

BUT – Contrast; the opposite

Romans 12:2

____

____

____

Conjunctions are words which link together multiple complete ideas. They focus on a specific kind of additive or contrasting relationship between the ideas.

Prepositions as Linking Words

A preposition describes a relationship between other words in a sentence. Typically, the preposition links a major idea (independent clause) with a secondary idea (dependent clause).

BECAUSE – for the reason that; what follows is a consequence of what precedes, linking

Ephesians 2:4-5

____

____

____

FOR – Indicate purpose/goal; with respect to; because, why

Ephesians 2:8-10

____

____

____

Other Words that Bear Noting

THEREFORE – Consequence of what came before

Hebrews 12:1

____

____

____

The same applies to other variants of this word such as wherefore. Therefore, always drives you back to the what came before. It may be referring to a single sentence, or to the contents of an entire chapter (or more!) that was written previously.

REPETITION – Using a word over and over throughout a passage

John:15:1-11

____

____

When you encounter a "therefore" in the text, ask "Wherefore is the therefore there for?" In other words, stop and take note of the word and identify what it is trying to communicate.

The Bible impacts your life right now!

How are you tempted to shortchange your study of the word of God?

Studying God's Word means getting into a level of details. What would hinder you from doing this?

____

____

A few tools were illustrated in this lesson; what would prevent you from learning more tools (e.g. grammar) so that you could better study God's word?

____

____

What rewards could you receive for pursuing this kind of detail in studying God's word?

____

____

05
Applying What You Learn

The study is incomplete until you apply it to your life

Simply Understanding is not Enough

The purpose of studying the Bible begins with understanding what the author is saying to their audience, but it does not stop there!

Understand what God is saying (comprehension) + Apply it to my life (application) Yields Grow & be transformed (transformation)

Studying the Bible without applying it will not result in the proper transformation and growth (milk to meat) that God intended. The different parts of this process are neither more nor less important that the others. What is important is that the ENTIRE process be completed to produce the correct result.

Proper application goes through a regular and repeatable set of steps:

Message Identification – what was the author trying to communicate to the original audience?

Audience mapping – how much is the original audience like me?

Message mapping – which elements of the message are relevant to me?

Action planning – what do I need to do in response?

Identify the Message

The last few lessons in this study have been focused on identifying the message. We have been over several techniques and tools such as:

- Author identification
- Audience identification
- Type of literature that is being used
- Establishing a context and working within that context

In addition, we have focused on tools which allow us to identify the actual message in a passage

- Paragraphs as containing a single main idea
- Sentences has having different types and purposes
- Key words that help reveal meaning.

The message is defined as what the original author communicated to the original readers.

These tools are designed to help us complete this first step in the application process. This step will probably take the bulk of the time of our study. Once the message has been identified, the rest of the application process can move forward.

Mapping the Audience

Key Principle: Identify how the original audience is like me (culturally, temporally, spiritually, etc.).

Leviticus 16:1-10

____

____

Psalms 1:1-2

____

____

Matthew 4:12-17

____

____

John 3:16

____

____

Galatians 5: 16-24

____

____

Mapping the Message

If the original audience is very distant from me, I can apply general principles. Some examples might include:

- What does the passage say about God, His character, His values and His plan?
- What does the people say about people in general, or the "human condition"?
- What are the characteristics of the way God relates to the people that are relevant today?

If the original audience is very similar to me, I can apply specific messages. Some examples might include:

- What actions does the passage call me to take?
- What does the passage forbid?
- How does the passage tell me I should behave?
- How does this passage exemplify the gospel?

If the original audience is neither distant nor similar, I can apply general principles and some specific messages.

- Any message that is specific to a way that the original audience is different than me cannot be applied directly
- Any general principle that is always true can still be applied

Mapping the Message

Key Principle: The more the audience is like me, the more directly God's message applies.

Leviticus 16:1-10

____

____

Psalms 1:1-2

____

____

Matthew 4:12-17

____

____

John 3:16

____

____

Galatians 5: 16-24

____

____

Plan for Action

James 1:22-25

____

____

We are called to act based on what we see in God's word.

Philippians 3:12-16

____

____

We press forward toward Jesus.

Philippians 1:3-11

____

____

It is Jesus (through the Holy Spirit) who produces the change.

Key Principle: Where God commands, I must obey. Where God forbids, I must avoid. What God likes; I must like. What God hates; I must hate.

The Bible impacts your life right now!

Do you let God's word have an impact in your life? Or do you make it stop at your head? The longest journey is often the 18 inches from your head to your heart!

What is the percentage of energy you spend identifying the meaning of a passage vs. applying it to your life? Is that the right split?

____

____

When you find an application, do you take it to heart, or just brush it off as inconsequential?

____

____

After you study the Bible, how much energy do you spend trying to take action on what has been applied?

____

____

____

06
The Six Easy Step Method

A repeatable process that will allow you to study scripture effectively

The Virtue of Investment

When studying the Bible, it's important to get a correct answer. But that does not mean you should simply go read what someone else has determined for the passage you're studying.

One of the key benefits of studying the Bible is the study process itself. It may seem difficult and confusing, and you might not get to an answer as quickly as you want. That's ok. The process of wrestling with God's word will pay dividends in your life.

The application you make will be many times more impactful if it represents work and effort to arrive at it. So don't think that you are wasting your time. You're not!!

Skill in studying the Bible comes with practice. And that means continuing to study even when you just want to get to the answer of "what should I do

If you lack confidence in your conclusions and applications, that's normal and to be expected. Keep doing what you're doing but find a Bible study partner where you can share your findings with them and discuss how they could be improved or corrected. It's ideal if that person is a little more experienced than you are – then they can provide tips and hints along the way.

Whatever you do, don't fall into the trap of looking up the answer in an external resource because you are not comfortable studying for yourself.

The Proper use of Study Bibles and Commentaries

Today's Bible student has more resources at their disposal than did many scholars several centuries ago. But not all resources are good for the beginning student. Resources have a specific place in the Bible study process and can be a great assist when used within those parameters.

2 Timothy 2:15 (a)

- Be diligent to present yourself approved to God (NASB)
- Study to shew thyself approved unto God (KJV)
- Do your best to present yourself to God as one approved (ESV)
- Work hard so you can present yourself to God and receive his approval (NLT)

What image or sense does this text evoke?

____

____

It is a proper biblical expectation that studying will take effort and energy and time. Only with much practice will it *appear* to be "easy". But for that student, the difficulty will have just moved to another level and new challenges will preset as old challenges are overcome.

The Six Easy Step Method

The Six Easy Step method is a repeatable process that can be used on virtually any passage of the Bible to accurately understand what God's Word means and says to you.

1. Read the text: Establish the author, audience, and context

2. Read the text: Identify the author's message

3. Identify questions you want to answer. Use your resources to find answers.

4. Read the text: Refine the author's message

5. Map the audience & message: Apply the message to your life

6. Compare your conclusions with others: Use any differences to expand your understanding

1. Establish Author, Audience and Context

Understanding who the **author** was provides critical insight into the nature of the communication, the style in which it was written and general guidance into the content that might be included.

Understanding the **audience** helps you understand what the need was that prompted the writing of the text. The audience also gives clues to their relationship with the author and often shapes the tone of the book.

Each part of the Bible exists in several layers of **context**. From the type of literature, to the relationship between the people to the size of the work, context shapes the message and ultimately the meaning.

2. Identify the Message (First Pass)

What does the passage say?

Spend your time examining the text itself. It will reveal the message to you.

- Look at the keywords – how do they shape meaning
- Look for contrast and comparison – what is the author trying to do?
- Look for commands or questions – they can show how the text is being summarized

During this step use your manuscript to make notes and highlights as needed to draw your attention to the point that the author is trying to make. This is one of the main reasons for creating a study manuscript in the first place. You can be as messy or wordy as you want. Your eyes are the main tool, but the manuscript is the canvas.

Summarize your findings in whatever format seems to be effective. Don't worry about being "right" yet. This is your preliminary step. You have more studying to do before you make a final determination.

3. Identify (and Answer) Questions

Asking questions is not a sign of weakness or ignorance. It is the first move of a curious mind that wants to know and learn. No question is too big. No question is too small.

The first step to learning is to formulate a question and write it down. As you go through Step 2, keep a list of things that you don't know which might make it easier to understand what the author is trying to communicate.

In Step 3, use your resources to find answers. This is where a few low-cost resources can make a tremendous difference in determining what the author says.

Just as you wrote the question down, write out your answer – it will stay in your study notes as documentation of your learning. The next time you come back to the study, you'll be able to see all the knowledge you've gained.

Without fail, once you've answered this batch of questions, when you come back, you'll find new questions. This is the sign of progress and growth.

4. Refine the Message

It may seem repetitive to return to the message of the passage a second time.

But this is a critical step. Since you've answered your questions, you will have fresh insight into the author's intentions and message.

Taking a break to do question research in Step 3 will also give your brain a chance to mull over what you've read. It can make fresh connections and insights.

Finally, another block of time understanding God's Word almost always produces new understanding. You may discover new content, or you may find a better way to summarize or organize your understanding.

Both are extremely valuable to the Bible Student.

Whenever you learn something new, come to the scriptures with fresh eyes. You have the chance to find fresh insight and revelation in God's word. With your questions now answered, you can see the passage anew and make fresh discoveries of what the author wants to say.

5. Map the Audience and Message

You've already mapped the audience in Step 1.

Review this mapping to decide if it's still relevant given your new knowledge. If you found multiple mappings, pick the one that applies best.

The closer the audience is to you, the more directly you can apply the message.

Map the message from the original audience to you.

The closer you are to the original audience, the more directly you can apply the message in your own life.

If you are distant to the audience, you'll need to step back from the direct message to find a more general application.

Apply the message and find the action to take.

The purpose of studying scripture is to find out out to live. That requires taking new or different actions.

If we read the Bible but don't do anything differently, then it will not have any power in our lives we will not be changed.

6. Compare your Conclusions

Begin at the beginning, not the ending!

It's tempting to jump into a study by reading what someone else has written or said based on their study. It seems like a great way to prepare.

All it does is spoil the learning process for you as a student. Save what other people have written and said until you have formed your own opinion from studying God's Word for yourself.

Reading other studies should always be saved for the last step.

There are many ways to compare what you learned

A great way is to study with a partner. At the end of each passage meet to review what you have learned and how you followed the steps. Seldom will 2 people see the same things or make the same conclusion. Comparison will offer a wonderful insight into other approaches.

A second method is to read a reliable commentary or published study to see how that author handled the text.

The Bible impacts your life right now!

Will you commit to following the process through all six steps? Shortcuts rarely are quicker paths to the desired destination. Each step has a purpose and contributes to the overall study outcome.

Consider the recommendations above; how many of them have you violated while trying to study God's word previously?

____

____

Do you have a suitable set of study resources? Will you commit to expanding your study library?

____

____

This book laid out a six-step approach to Bible study. Will you commit to using it to study a passage of the Bible in the next two weeks?

____

____

07
Bible Study Resources for You

Choosing the right resource can make a difference in your study

Building your Study Library

Resources are used to answer specific questions that arise out of the text which we cannot answer with our personal knowledge.

- When was this written?
- What does that word mean?
- Who is that person and what did they do?
- What is the audience's greatest need?
- What else was going on when this was written?

Building a Study Library doesn't have to be a big investment. There are a few relatively inexpensive resources that can make a tremendous difference in your personal Bible study

Some of these resources are virtually free and can be found at an office supply shop. Others are published books that will provide trustworthy information at your fingertips.

Start with what you can but commit to grow your study library over time. It's an investment that will pay tremendous dividends over the course of the rest of your study life.

Resource 1: Paper and Pen

Believe it or not, your eyes and a pen or pencil are the most important resource you'll find!

Get a fresh look at the passage by copying it into your favorite word processing application. Use the formatting to give it wide margins and generous spacing. Then read over it a few times to get the sense of what is being said. Use paragraph format so you can group together the main ideas and supporting text.

Then use a pen or pencil to note questions that occur to you while you are reading. Just put them in the margin. Highlight important or repeated words. Sometimes they will show a pattern throughout the text.

Sometimes it's helpful to get the text out of your Bible. Many Bibles today have small print and cramped margins, so there is a very limited opportunity to be able to put your thoughts and questions on the page.

As you learn more about the passage, jot this down too! When you are done, this printed copy will become an invaluable resource of information on the passage,. Not only that, but all your notes will remind you of the learning and discovery process you followed to be able to come to some conclusions.

It can be very beneficial to go back and look at old study notes and see how much you've learned and recall the discover process again.

Resource 2: Study Bible

Suggested Options:

ESV Study Bible

Ryrie Study Bible

John MacArthur Study Bible

NIV Zondervan Study Bible

Study Bibles are chock-full of useful resources that can really help.

A good study bible is a treasure trove of useful resources. Whether you are looking for help on a specific passage, or if you want to expand your knowledge of Bible study, your Study Bible will have a great set of tools for taking you deeper.

- Cross- references
- Maps & Diagrams
- Book overviews/introductions
- Resource materials
- Cross Reference Notes
- Notes, explanations & commentary

Take some time to review all the reference materials that are available in your study Bible. Don't just look within the text of the scripture. Most study Bibles have significant materials at the end or beginning too.

Resource 3: Bible Dictionary

A Bible dictionary offers an alphabetized list of words with definitions and explanations.

A Bile dictionary won't explain the meaning of a given passage of scripture, but it will give you background on many of the things you read about in your Bible. A Bible dictionary is a useful resource when trying to answer questions that arise out of reading the path. You will find that the dictionary has useful background and explanatory information on many different people, places, events and objects.

Recommended

Do you want a brief biography of Naaman? An overview of the Galilee region of Israel? A summary of the Babylonian conquest of Jerusalem? Or perhaps an explanation of what is a synagogue? A Bible dictionary will have entries on all these items that will provide you with a brief background and overview so you can better understand them as they occur in the passage.

Resource 4: Bible Handbook

Recommended

A Bible handbook offers a background and insight into passages of scripture.

A Bible handbook is like a Bible dictionary, except in stead of being organized alphabetically by topic, it is organized by the order of passages in the Bible. The Bible Handbook will provide a significant amount of information to introduce each of the 66 books (like your study bible, but perhaps in more detail), Additionally the handbook will offer background regarding different paragraphs in the passage itself.

It would be interesting to think that the Bible handbook provides the entire study for a given passage in the Bible. However, the real purpose is to gain insight into what the passage is talking about so that you can draw your own conclusions based on what the text says, rather than what the handbook says.

Resource 5: Theology & Doctrine

A systematic theology book provides you with in-depth topical information about the various doctrines of the Christian faith.

As you encounter different topics throughout your study, you might want to know more about their theological and doctrinal perspectives. A book of Systematic Theology presents these materials in an effective way to understand what we believe on the topic and how it relates to other topics and doctrines.

A book of theology and doctrine is a tremendous resource as you dig into different theological topics. Not only will it address the scope of the theology, but also variations and their origins, as well as discussions of different considerations and angles to consider. A good Systematic Theology will be loaded with scriptural references so you can link the material back to what God says.

Recommended

The Internet is NOT a Resource

Several Bible-based websites can be very useful and have been proven trustworthy over time.

Blue Letter Bible
blb.org

Bible Gateway
biblegateway.com

Logos Bible Software
logos.com

While the internet is tempting and easy to access, it is the breeding ground of heresy, ignorance, misinformation and bad theology.

The internet is full of people you do not know, who have not been verified or validated. Their theology and teaching has not been tested and found to be good. You do not know whether you are getting truth or lies from them. Assume lies.

While it may be tempting to use a search engine to look for information on the internet, this is not a valid study technique. All the materials recommended in this book have been reviewed and found to be trustworthy. The same cannot be said of resources found on the internet.

Unless you receive a recommendation from a mature believer, you should be skeptical about anything you find there.

The Bible impacts your life right now!

Have you ever run directly to a study resource instead of going straight to God's Word? How will you change your approach going forward?

____

____

How have you used commentaries in your study process up until now? After reading this chapter, do you think you've used the best approach or a shortcut approach?

____

____

Do you have a suitable set of resources at home that will support an effective study of the Bible? Will you commit to expanding your resources?

____

____

Do you use resources properly or are they a shortcut to an easy answer that avoids the work of digging in yourself?

08
How To Start Your Study

Taking the right first step is essential to following the study process

Breaking Down the Study

Setting the context requires a dedicated focus and process.

It is critical to begin to develop an understanding of the entire book being studied. This overview forms a foundation for the detailed study that comes later. The first step in the Six Easy Steps process focuses exclusively on this context.

Detailed study of smaller parts comes later.

You get to choose how much text to study in one study session. You may take several settings to complete the session. The is completed when all six steps have been completed for the indicated section of the Bible.

For starters, study a chapter in each session.

In most books of the Bible, a single chapter is a good-sized unit of study.

As you gain experience and confidence, you can define other units, such as groups of paragraphs or sets of verses as your study unit.

The Getting Started Process

Establishing Author, Audience & Context:

1. Read the book and **identify the author** and everything they reveal about themselves

2. Read the book and **identify the audience** and everything revealed about them

3. Read the book and **highlight or mark keywords** that jump out of the text at you

4. Read the book and **summarize each paragraph** with 1-3 keywords from the paragraph

5. **Make a list of questions** that you have based on what you've read

6. Write out in **one sentence or a brief paragraph what you currently understand the book to be about**.

While the Six Easy Steps method features six steps, getting started focuses on the first step. We will break it down into six detailed sub-steps and allocate one entire study session to identifying author, audience and the context.

Step 1.1 Identify the Author

Read the entire book and note everything the author reveals about themself.

If you created a study manuscript, use a pen or colored pencils to highlight the sections.

What should you pay attention to?

Does the author introduce themselves?

Does the author share any information about their current circumstances?

Does the author share any prior experience with the audience or their setting/location?

Does the author refer to any other people or locations?

Does the author describe their emotional state in writing the book?

Does the author use any personal examples to make their point?

Does the author explain why they are writing?

Step 1.2 Identify the Audience

What should you pay attention to?

Does the author introduce or name their audience?

Does the author say anything about where the audience is located?

Does the author share any details about the circumstances the audience is in?

Does the author reference any audience members by name?

Does the author describe a problem the audience is experiencing?

Does the author refer to any history between themselves and the audience?

Read the entire book and note everything the author reveals about their audience.

If you created a study manuscript, use a pen or colored pencils to highlight the sections.

Step 1.3 Identify Keywords

Read the entire book and note any key words that seem to have special importance.

If you created a study manuscript, use a pen or colored pencils to mark the words so they are more visible.

When marking a manuscript, it's helpful to make a key so you know what words or concepts you're tracking and how they are marked. Write down the word and mark it how it will be identified in the text.

The keywords could be those outlined in Chapter 4. You can also highlight words that are repeated, or words which seem to be important or stand out to you as you read over the chapter.

Step 1.4 Summarize Paragraphs

In most books, paragraphs make meaningful building blocks

In longer books you could use other structural units such as entire chapters. You could also read the book and identify logical sections that flow though the book.

A paragraph summary is a special technique. When we looked at paragraphs in Chapter Four, we said that every paragraph has a theme sentence. When you summarize the paragraph, you'll want to identify that theme and represent it in one or two key words, ideally taken from the sentence itself.

By summarizing paragraphs, we'll gain a birds-eye view of the entire book. The message of the book is the sum of the messages of the paragraphs.. In twenty words or less, you'll have a quick overview.

A paragraph summary should be short and to the point. Shoot for no more than three words to make the summary. Whenever possible, use important words from the paragraph itself in the summary.

This is a skill that takes practice and time, so don't become frustrated if it doesn't come naturally at first.

Step 1.5 Make a List of Questions (and Answers)

As you read the book, you might uncover some questions.

By writing them down , you'll free up your brain to leave them alone for a while,.

If you're ready with some resources, you can start to do some research now. Try to limit your research to only answer the questions lest you start to get biased by outside influences..

Questions aren't a sign of ignorance.

Asking questions is a normal method for identifying what you want to learn. Writing down the question forces you to be specific about what you want to know. So don't be afraid to write down many questions.

Summary level questions can be researched and answered here. Specific questions can be saved for the more detailed study.

Step 1.6 Summarize your Understanding

Writing the summary isn't about producing a work of art. It's a functional tool to help you see what you've already learned from your study.

Elements to consider using in your summary:

- Who is the author?
- Who did they write to and what is the relationship between them?
- What is the setting of the book?
- What is the reason for writing the book?
- What key point or points are made?

Summarize

Write out a short overview of the book. You should include the results of each of the steps that you've just gone through.

The summary doesn't have to be in pretty sentences. But it should represent what you've learned about the book.

Getting Started Review

Don't be in a hurry to finish.

As you start your study, don't be in a race to "get to the good stuff". Part of following the Six Easy Step method is progressively diving deeper and deeper into the book.

The value of this summary step cannot be overstated. Without it you run the risk of moving into the book and getting lost in the authors objective and method.

Start Right

Spending time establishing the right context for the book you're studying is a great way to lay out the framework for a successful study. As you progressively dive deeper into the study, this first step will help you stay focused on what the author was trying to communicate.

09
How To Do A Chapter Study

A repeatable process for any study

Getting Ready for a Chapter Study

Get ready by reviewing your notes

Go back over your notes from the study overview step. Look at the message for the entire book and note what parts of that message are associated with each chapter.

Take a moment to review your manuscript and see if you marked any keywords or other observations that will help you dig deeper into the chapter.

Now you're ready to dig into the Six-Step study process!

1. Read the text and identify Author, Audience, Context

2. Read the Text and identify the Author's message

3. Identify questions you want to answer.

4. Read the text and refine the Author's message

5. Map the Audience and message

6. Compare your conclusions with others

The detailed study process builds on the foundation of the overview. Each chapter is clearer when you understand what the book is trying to accomplish as a complete unit.

Reviewing Step 1

You completed Step 1 (Author, Audience, Context) in the overview. This gave you a bird's-eye book of the entire book.

As you start the detailed study of each chapter, go back to your overview notes and review what you wrote down.

Take some time to review the chapter again and identify which elements of the overview occur within the chapter you're about to study. Pay attention to see if any new observations appear for you.

Look at the paragraph summaries, keywords you've highlighted, and any notes you've already made.

Think about author trying to communicate to the audience and how he might have wanted to approach the topics in this chapter.

You might even spend some time looking for new patterns in words or ideas.

Following Steps 2, 3 & 4

Detailed steps for this part of the study was covered in detail in Chapter 6: The Six Easy Step Method. Refer to that chapter for an in-depth review of those steps.

When conducting your study, you will follow steps 2, 3 and 4 exactly as they are explained in Chapter 6

2. Read the text: Identify the author's message. This is your preliminary understanding. As the study progresses, you'll be able to refine it.

3. Identify questions you want to answer. Use your resources to find answers. Write out both your questions and answers.

4. Read the text: Refine the author's message. This is the result of all the study that has happened previously and represents what you believe the author was trying to communicate to the original audience.

Performing Step 5

You did a preliminary mapping of the audience in the Overview study.

As you look at the chapter under study, you will want to review the mapping you did before and determine how it applies to this chapter. Did you did you identify multiple possible mappings? Then pick the one which is most appropriate based on the contents of this chapter.

Once you've decided how to map the audience you can make the appropriate mapping of the message. Adjust the message by making it specific or more generic depending on the closeness of the audience.

Example:

In the book of Titus, we can map Titus as very close to us as a New Testament Christian.

We can also map him as a church leader operating under the direction of an Apostle. For most lay believers, who are not church leaders, this would be a more distant mapping, and would require some adjustment to the message to account for that.

Wrapping up with Step 6

Find a Study Buddy

One of the best ways to study the Bible is with a partner. Each of you studies the text on your own and then meets to compare notes. Having a partner who is going through the process with you can be a tremendous help as they will be able to provide options for you when you get stuck.

Who could you ask?

Use Resources

If you have been building a study library, you can use some of your resources to compare your results. Whether you read the notes in your Study Bible, look at the information in a Bible Handbook or review a trusted Bible commentary, this is a good way to gain further insight on what you've studied.

What if you don't have either?

It's not the end of the world. If you don't have anyone or anything to compare to, just skip this step. It won't hurt your study.

Alternatively, you could talk to a pastor at your church to see if they can provide you with someone who could serve as a mentor to talk to you about your study.

Wrap Up

As you study the Bible, you will work through all six steps of the study method.

You will repeat this process for every study unit. In the beginning, it's probably best to use a chapter as the basis of setting a study unit. But it's up to you to decide how to define your study unit.

Because some of the work will have been at least started in the Getting Started process, you'll need to review those results in Step 1 and Step 5 to remind you of what you've already decided and see if your detailed study has any additional information to add.

Finally, the best practice is to compare your results to get a different perspective. But if you don't have someone or a resource to use, you can skip this step.

Set a timeframe.

Each study unit should be competed in a specific timeframe. It's not good to get stuck in a chapter and stay there for too long.

So, determine how long you want to spend on each chapter and when the time has expired, move on.

One week is a good rule of thumb for the time to spend on each chapter.

10
How To Finish Your Study

Finish strong to realize the most impact

Pairing the Overview with the Conclusion

When evaluating a book to study, you can estimate the number of study sessions it will take by counting the number of chapters and adding 2 additional sessions for the Overview and the Conclusion.

Looking at the book of Titus, it contains 3 chapters, so we would expect a total of 5 study units.

Setting a timeframe of 1 week per study unit leads to a total timeline of 5 weeks.

Just as we began the Bible book study with an overview step, we want to finish with a Summary step.

When the Holy Spirit inspired the author to write the book, He inspired the entire book. So now that we've gone through the book in detail, chapter by chapter, it's time to step back and review the entire book.

The summary step ties up the whole study by looking at the biggest messages which connect through the entire book.

The Six Summary Steps

1. Review the book and identify any **major sections** that you now see in the book

2. Review the previous study units and **summarize** what the book has to say

3. Write a **single sentence** that summarizes the theme or the purpose of the book

4. Identify a **single verse** which provides the key to the book

5. Considering the way you've mapped the audience, what's **one application** that comes out of the book?

6. **Compare** your conclusions with others

Wrapping up follows its own process. For every study you have six steps that will take you through the process of summarizing your study and finding the biggest and most important points and application to use.

Step 1: Identify Major Sections

You decide how you want to define a section. It's your summary of the book. The structure should be based on your study and what you've learned.

Sections represent your understanding of the book.

Now that you've studied the entire book, identify the way that you see it grouped together. You probably will have studied the book chapter by chapter, but now that the detailed study is complete, you might have identified other ways that the author grouped or organized their thoughts.

Write out your key sections and provide the references for each section.

If you ever come back to the study later, you will be able to refer to this learning and potentially reshape the way you study the book in the future.

Step 2: Summarize the Message

Summarizing the messages in the book focuses on what the author said in the book. It is different from the structure of how the author organized their ideas.

You will find a close relationship between Steps 1 and 2. Structure influences content and vice versa. So, work carefully through these two steps.

As you summarize, reflect on the sections that you identified in Step 1. How do those sections influence the way that you express your summary.

As an alternative you could also summarize each section and see if that helps you complete the whole-book summary.

Step 3: Write a Summary Sentence

In the Overview process you wrote out a one sentence summary of the entire book. Now that the book study is complete, write another summary sentence of the entire book that reflects your deeper knowledge gained during the study.

Summarizing your book study can be challenging because you now know so much more about the book.

The objective is to look at the sections and the message and find the parts that are the MOST IMPORTANT to the book. Go with those ideas.

You should shoot for a single sentence. But if you can't do that, two sentences is acceptable. Remember you won't be able to cover all the details. So go for the big picture.

Step 4: Identify the Key Verse

A key verse is the verse that speaks to the entire book.

It could be a verse that describes why the book was written.

It could be a verse that offers a summary of what the entire book is about.

It could be a verse that expresses the biggest point of the book.

It could be a verse that serves as a pivot point for the book.

Choosing the verse and owning the reason you picked it is the hard work of this step. You may come to the book with many verses that stand out. But this assignment means narrowing it down to one verse.

Step 5: Identify the Whole-Book Application

"We learn to live." We learn something so that we can apply it to our lives and live differently, better, giving more glory to God, better pursuing the mission He has assigned us here on earth.

Unless the Bible changes your life, it's not doing you any good. That's why we study the bible with an eye to applying it to our lives.

Looking back over all the applications and actions that you wrote down, is there one that most applies to you and represents the transformation the book brought?

Alternatively, looking at the entire book, you might map the meaning and produce a new application that serves as the takeaway for the entire book.

Write out the application that you are taking away from the whole book. What action does it compel you to take. Without action, there will be no change or transformation.

Step 6: Compare Your Conclusions

Work with a friend or a partner to study God's Word.

Having a study buddy will help you get the most out of your study. Not only can they help when you encounter problems, but as they share their study results, you'll gain additional insight on the book where they came to different conclusions.

If you don't have a partner, you can use a resource or book.

Perhaps you have a commentary on the book. Perhaps your Bible Handbook has a good discussion of the book.

These resources won't help with an application, but they can help you refine your understanding of the book.

Wrap Up

The purpose of the wrap up is to help you see the message and the purpose of the entire Bible book.

When you complete the study, it can be a confidence boost to compare your wrap up notes with your overview notes. You should see a dramatically different level of knowledge and understanding in the wrap up. This is the accumulated benefit of the study that you have completed.

Save your study notes, including the wrap up, so that you can come back later and review your study. For a real treat, come back in a couple years and study the book again and see what more you can learn!

Finishing the study doesn't happen when you study the last verse in the book. The wise Bible student looks back on what they have done to see the lessons learned and how they build toward changing a life.

What Next?

Put what you've learned into practice

Where will you go from here?

Congratulations on completing the materials in this book!

This brings you to a new beginning, not an end. The information in this book is designed to prepare you for studying the Bible. Now the entire Bible is open before you.

I've prepared a simple 6-week study of the book **Titus**.

We'll go through the same process that you've just learned. I'll be your study buddy and share all my notes for Step 6 so you can see how I approached the study.

And if you ever have a question, I'm just an email away!

The study is designed to work over email. Each week I'll send you the instructions for the study unit. I've also included a few bonus tools that I think you'll find helpful and interesting.

At the end of each week, I'll send you my study notes and explain what I was thinking as I studied that unit.

How to Start your Study of Titus

Scan this QR code in the camera of your cell phone and it will take you to a sign-up page.

Or you can go to my website by typing this address in your browser:

https://Dennis-Stevenson.com/StudyTitus

On the web page, sign up by entering your name and email address. I'll send you a welcome email right away and you'll be set!

Here's the agenda we'll follow.

Week 1: Getting Ready
Week 2: Introduction
Week 3: Titus Chapter 1
Week 4: Titus Chapter 2
Week 5: Titus Chapter 3
Week 6: Wrap Up

Titus is a Great Starter-Study

Facts about Titus:

Author: Paul

Audience: Titus

Chapters: 3

Timeline: 1st Century

Topics: Christian living in a time of false teachers.

The next step is a study of the book of Titus.

You might not be familiar with this book of the Bible. That's OK. Titus is a great starter study for several reasons:

1. **It's Short**. When starting out, it's best to take an easy first step. Length of the book is one of the factors that adds difficulty to a study.

2. **It's written to an individual**. Some books of the Bible have an ambiguous audience. Or they are written to a group of people. Titus is written to a church leader named Titus. This helps keep it more focused.

3. **It's simple and practical**. Paul has a few direct points to make. This makes understanding easier.

All you need to do is sign up!

Congratulations!

Now you've completed the entire study. You've learned how to study your Bible and I hope you've signed up to start your first study.

Don't let time slip way before you reinforce what you've just learned. What would you like to study next?

Let me know at Dennis@Dennis-Stevenson.com

www.ingramcontent.com/pod-product-compliance
Lightning Source LLC
Chambersburg PA
CBHW081223130726
47997CB00009B/2757